From Zero to Game Designer

An Essential Guide

Table of Contents

Chapter 1. Introduction

In an exciting landscape where creativity meets technology, everyone can have a shot at making their dream game a reality! Our Special Report titled, "From Zero to Game Designer: An Essential Guide" is exactly the ladder you need to climb the echelons of game development. Whether you're a budding creative itching to express your innovative game ideas, an enthusiast seeking a career shift, or a seasoned programmer brimming with game projects, this guide is your golden ticket. Filled with inspirations, secrets from industry veterans, and user-friendly technical breakdowns, this guide is the springboard that will catapult you into the exhilarating world of game design. Dive in, and let's turn your game dreams into game-changing realities!

Chapter 2. Exploring the Landscape of Game Design

Game design is an art as much as it is a science, an intricate blend of creative storytelling, sophisticated design, and complex programming. It's a vast landscape, with myriad opportunities and avenues for exploration, but knowing where to start can be challenging. This chapter is designed to guide you through that landscape, providing you with an understanding of what game design entails, the various roles within the industry, the skills required, and the process of game development. It will also offer insights into the current trends and future prospects.

2.1. The Essentials of Game Design

The game design process is multi-faceted and involves various stages from concept creation to game testing. It requires a basic understanding of systems development, the ability to weave engaging stories, character development, level creation, and great visual design balance. All these, coupled with a robust understanding of the technical aspects of game programming, contribute to effective game design.

When creating a game, designers start with a concept. This could be a simple idea or an elaborate narrative. The idea is then conceptualized into game mechanics, including character design, level creation, rules, and goal setting. Making a game requires a lot of problem solving and team collaboration, as development teams often comprise individuals with different skillsets. Their collective contribution defines the final product's success.

Further, how the user interacts with a game (user experience - UX) and how it looks (user interface - UI) is another critical aspect of game design. It determines how players perceive and enjoy your game, influencing its acceptance. Designing a game involves detailed planning, curating the perfect balance between complexity and fun.

2.2. Roles in the Game Design Industry

You can wear many hats in the game design industry. The core team usually consists of the following roles, each of which is critical to the project's successful completion:

1. Game Designer: Think of this role as the game's conductor. Their core responsibility is to ensure that all game features work collectively to provide an enjoyable and immersive player experience.

2. Concept Artist: They are responsible for creating the game's visual style. This involves designing characters, environments, objects, and often even the storyboard.

3. Programmer: Without programmers, our game concepts and artworks are just theoretical. They bring the game to life, making all its elements workable and interactive.

4. Level Designer: They map out the game's progression, designing each level's layout and challenge.

5. Story Writer/Narrative Designer: Games need compelling stories and engaging dialogues. The Story Writer or Narrative Designer weaves the plot, captivating players through a well-crafted narrative.

6. Sound Designer: They create the game's audio aspects, from effects to music, which play a key role in maintaining the atmosphere and game's overall vibe.

7. QA Tester: They are the game's first actual players and are critical in identifying bugs, inconsistencies, and aspects of the game that can be improved for the end player.

While there are more specialized roles as per the needs of a project, these form the backbone of any game design team.

2.3. Skills Required in Game Design

As varied as the roles in the game design industry, so are the required skills. However, some fundamental skills remain critical to succeeding in any game design role:

1. Creativity and Imagination: Games are a form of expression, and the best games often come from out-of-the-box thinking and innovative ideas.

2. Technical Skills: Depending on the role, this could be proficiency in programming languages, familiarity with game engines, understanding UX/UI design, or using graphic design software.

3. Problem Solving: Game designing is about finding solutions to interactive problems, be it designing a level or figuring out how to bring a particular idea to life.

4. Teamwork: As already stated, game design is a team effort. The ability to work well in a team and collaborate with other professionals is crucial to a game designer's role.

5. Attention to Details: Games are made up of a multitude of details, each contributing to the overall player experience. Hence, a keen eye for details is beneficial in this industry.

6. Understanding of Player Psychology: This understanding helps designers create compelling and engaging user experiences.

2.4. The Game Design Process

Designing a game is not a linear process, but it typically starts with an idea. This idea then undergoes several iterations, evolving into a playable game. Here's a typical workflow:

1. Conceptualization: This stage involves brainstorming and developing the general idea for the game. This could be a story, a mechanic, a theme, or a mix of elements.

2. Prototyping: Here, designers create rudimentary versions of the game, testing the concept and its mechanics.

3. Designing: Depending on the feedback, designers create the architecture of the game, flesh out the story, characters, levels, and so on.

4. Development: This is where everything comes together. Programmers code the game, artists fashion the visuals, level designers create the stages, and so on.

5. Testing: The game is tested for bugs, performance issues, and player engagement. Feedback from this phase informs improvements or bug fixes.

6. Launch: Game is released for players to enjoy.

7. Post-Launch: Most games require maintenance post-launch. This could include updates, new features, bug fixes, and more.

2.5. Trends and Future of the Game Design Industry

We are in the golden age of video games, with new technologies consistently transforming the industry. The advent of VR and AR, for example, has opened up new dimensions of gaming. Mobile gaming is exploding, while indie games with their innovative mechanics and narratives are gaining popularity. Esports is another budding sector that's driving the industry forward. With continuous innovations, the future is exciting and promising for young game designers.

In conclusion, game design is an exciting field with a lot to offer. It's a landscape that encourages creativity and innovation while being quite rewarding at the same time. As we've seen in this chapter, it calls for a broad range of skills and an in-depth understanding of the process, but this complexity is part of its charm. As you step into the game design world, remember - the player is at the heart of all you do, and their continued engagement is your ultimate success.

Chapter 3. How to Establish a Solid Foundation in Programming

Beginning on this essential path into the world of game development, the first and most fundamental step involves establishing a solid foundation in programming. Programming is the backbone of any game project, providing developers with the power to bring their creative visions to life through interactive and dynamic experiences.

3.1. Understanding Programming Basics

Before delving deep into the intricacies of game-specific programming, it is critical to master the basics of general programming. Programming is a way of giving instructions to computers, telling them what to do, when, and how. It involves writing scripts in specific languages that a computer can interpret and execute.

To begin this learning journey, it's recommended to select a beginner-friendly language. Python, for instance, is often rated as an excellent starting point given its simplicity and the availability of countless resources for learning. The choice of the programming language usually depends on the nature of the project or the demands of the software you wish to create. However, rest assured that the fundamental concepts are transferable from one language to another.

In the early stages, you should focus on:

1. Learning syntax - The set of rules that define how programs

written in a language must be structured.

2. Understanding variables, data types, and operators - These are the basic building blocks of any program.

3. Grasping the essentials of control flow - Including loops (for, while), and conditional statements (if, else).

4. Learning about functions - Reusable blocks of code that perform a specific task.

Revisit these concepts frequently and practice them with plenty of exercises to ensure a thorough understanding and assimilation.

3.2. Digging Into Object-Oriented Programming

After grasping the basics, the next step is understanding Object-Oriented Programming (OOP). Guided by four main principles – encapsulation, inheritance, polymorphism, and abstraction – OOP allows you to structure your software in a sustainable and efficient manner.

OOP exceptionally shines in game development. For instance, if you are creating a racing game, each car can be an object with properties (like speed, color) and methods (like accelerate, brake). Such a structure can help you manage a complex game world with numerous entities and interactions.

3.3. Intro to Game Programming

Having established a strong foundation in general programming, it's time to dive into game-specific programming. This specialized discipline varies significantly from typical software development because games are real-time systems that require high performance and responsiveness.

One key principle you need to explore is the game loop - the core structure of any game that's responsible for executing gameplay functions in the correct order and managing time properly. Every single game, whether a simple 2D platformer or a complex 3D RPG, fundamentally runs on this game loop principle.

Master inputs, as they trigger character actions like jumping, shooting, or relocating. Also, grasping the basics of Artificial Intelligence (AI) is beneficial as it's behind the non-player characters' behaviour in the game.

3.4. Getting Hands-on with Game Development Tools

Real game development starts when you begin working with game engines – software that simplifies creating games by offering features such as graphics rendering, physics engines, and AI functionalities, amongst others.

One of the most popular game engines is Unity, known for its powerful features and versatility. Unity uses C#, a statically-typed language that shares characteristics with both C and Java. Besides Unity, there's Unreal Engine (uses C), Godot (uses GDScript, similar to Python), and many others.

Remember, while choosing an engine, factors to consider include your proficiency in the supported programming language, the platform you want to develop for, and the type of game you want to make (2D, 3D, VR, etc.).

3.5. Learning by Doing

The ultimate secret to establishing a solid foundation in programming is practice. Take on small projects, contribute to open-source games, create mods, or experiment with game jams. Every bit of practice will add to your skills and make you a more proficient programmer.

Programming principles can be daunting at times, but remember, the best game developers were once beginners too. Don't let rough patches deter you; instead, reach out to communities, take breaks when needed, and keep the fire of curiosity alive.

By putting in time and effort, consistently learning and practising, you'll find yourself gradually evolving into a proficient game developer with a solid foundation in programming. Now, buckle up and get ready for the next chapter of your game development journey!

Chapter 4. Mastering Essential Game Design Tools

Whether you're fine-tuning a character's dynamic movement or constructing expansive and immersive worlds, the right set of tools in your utility belt can elevate your game design process. This segment aims to provide you a wider understanding of the fundamental game design tools, their relevance, and an overview on how to utilize them.

4.1. Software Development Kits

Software Development Kits (SDKs) are fundamental elements in game development. They provide essential frameworks and libraries that facilitate building and optimizing runtime components, simplifying processes in the system-level groundwork.

1. **Unity**: Unity is predominantly used for developing both two-dimensional (2D) and three-dimensional (3D) games and simulations. It is written in C# language and can export games to 27 different platforms. It also supports drag-and-drop functionality, making it user-friendly for beginners. Unity also offers a plethora of tutorials and extensive documentation, so one never has to fret about troubleshooting.

2. **Unreal Engine**: Unreal Engine is known for its high-end graphics capabilities and is widely used in the development of AAA games. Compatible with VR, it opens the doors to developing immersive gameplay experiences. This engine possesses a visual scripting tool, Blueprint, which makes the engine more approachable for beginners and non-programmers.

3. **Godot**: Godot is open-source software and a powerful tool for both 2D and 3D game development. Its uniqueness stems from its scene and node system, which provides an organized method of

creating games. It supports both visual scripting and full language scripting in C# and GDScript.

4.2. Graphic Design Software

The visual aspect is a crucial element that captures a player's interest. Utilize the power of innovative software to create striking visuals and add depth to your character and environment design.

1. **Adobe Photoshop**: This tool empowers you to create and modify images at pixel level, offering extensive editing and layering options which are ideal for designing game textures, backgrounds, and characters.

2. **Blender**: Blender is a free open-source 3D modeling tool. With this, you can create any 3D asset for your game, from characters to scenery. Blender supports the entire 3D pipeline—modeling, rigging, animation, simulation, rendering, compositing and motion tracking, and 2D animation.

3. **SketchUp**: SketchUp is used for its swift prototyping capabilities and simplicity in user interface. It is popular among game designers for creating environments and architecture.

4.3. Audio Design Software

Sound is a fundamental element in creating an immersive gaming experience. It establishes the mood and heightens gameplay.

1. **Audacity**: A free, open-source, and robust audio software that can record, edit, and mix audio tracks, Audacity provides an excellent platform for beginners to start with the basics of sound design.

2. **FMOD**: FMOD facilitates more complex audio operations. It has a Studio tool for creating high-quality sound effects and has a run-time API for audio implementation in multiple platforms.

Integrations with game development platforms like Unity and Unreal Engine is an added advantage.

3. **GarageBand**: GarageBand offers an intuitive interface for creating, editing, and implementing sound files. Initially aimed at music production, it has now gained popularity among game developers for crafting game soundtracks, dialogue, and sound effects.

With these tools, you can breathe life into your ideas, creating captivating and unforgettable gaming experiences. Take time to explore and familiarize yourself with each of these tools, understand their capabilities, pros and cons, and you would be one step closer to becoming a pro game designer. As you keep navigating the dynamic labyrinth of game design, remember there's no ultimate "best" tool - the best one is indeed what best suits you, your work style, and your game goals. Grasp these tools and wield them as a master craftsman, to shape a game that resonates with your vision.

Chapter 5. Understanding Mechanics, Dynamics and Aesthetics

Game design, at its core, is comprised of three fundamental components: mechanics, dynamics, and aesthetics. Understanding this trinity is key in producing a game that's not only fun to play, but also engaging and memorable.

5.1. Mechanics: The Rules of the Game

The mechanics of a game dictate how the game world functions and how players interact within that world. Mechanics can include aspects like game rules, character abilities, item functions, environmental interactions, and progression systems. Essentially, mechanics encompass all the interactive components of a game that enable players to engage with the game world.

For starters, consider chess. The game board, pieces, and choice of moves: these all make up the mechanics. It's the foundation upon which the game is built, playing a pivotal role in defining the player experience. Chess wouldn't be chess without its rules for piece movement and capture.

Understanding and employing game mechanics effectively is crucial to creating an engaging player experience. It requires detailed planning and tireless iteration to ensure every mechanic is working harmoniously and serving its intended purpose. Game mechanics should be compelling, fostering a sense of curiosity and engagement. They should encourage exploration and strategic decision-making.

Exploring different types of mechanics can lead to the creation of unique experiences that stand out from the crowd. Platform games allow players to jump around from platform to platform, puzzle mechanics see players solving conundrums, and strategies demand players manage resources and make decisions impacting the wider game world.

5.2. Dynamics: The Players' Moves

Dynamics are the patterns and behaviors that emerge from gameplay as a result of the mechanics. Simply put, if mechanics are the rules, dynamics are the gameplay that those rules foster. In chess, the strategies that unfold during gameplay exemplify dynamics.

Capturing the queen, setting up a defensive wall of pieces, or advancing pawns to distract the opponent – these are all dynamics brought about by the mechanics of chess. Dynamics involve anything that players do or can do in reaction to game mechanics.

Dynamics can be straightforward or complex, depending on the mechanics they stem from. For instance, a simple jumping mechanic may lead to dynamic platforming sequences, while a mechanic involving complex resource management may lead to a dynamic market system.

Keep in mind that dynamics often emerge unexpectedly and unpredictably from simple mechanics. Even the smallest mechanical adjustment can ripple and forever change the dynamics of your game, something designers should be mindful of during the iterative process.

5.3. Aesthetics: The Player Experience

Aesthetics, in terms of game design, doesn't merely relate to the visual aspect of the game. Essentially, aesthetics are how the game feels to the player, including emotional reactions and responses to the game. They're the reasons why a player might enjoy a game, and they give the game its flavor and appeal.

Chess, in terms of aesthetics, is often described as intellectual, competitive, and strategic. The feelings of intensity and rivalry, the satisfaction from a well-executed strategy, or the suspenseful anticipation of an opponent's move, all paint the aesthetic of chess.

For game designers, understanding and effectively leveraging aesthetics can be the difference between a good game and a great one. Aesthetics can create emotional resonance, foster player immersion, and encourage compelling gameplay. This includes everything from the look, sound, and feel of the game to how it challenges a player and elicits emotional responses.

Take, for instance, the popular game "Minecraft." Its unique blocky aesthetic is instantly recognizable and has been key to its enduring popularity, acting as a springboard for player creativity.

5.4. Crafting the Perfect Trinity

A well-balanced blend of mechanics, dynamics, and aesthetics is key to creating a successful game. Where mechanics provide the platform for interaction, dynamics extend this into a complex web of behaviors and strategies, and aesthetics create the emotional context that drives these behaviors.

It's easy to think of these aspects in isolation, but they exist in symbiosis. Each feeds into the other, and shifts in one can cause ripples in the others. For instance, changing a mechanic can alter the dynamics, prompting change in aesthetics, and vice versa.

Your understanding of these three aspects and their interplay will profoundly affect the quality of your game design. Balance them, and you have a game that's engaging, dynamic, and aesthetically pleasing, a game that's not just fun to play, but also compelling and memorable.

5.5. Understanding Through Prototyping

There's no substitute for practical experience. Working on a prototype will give you intimate, hands-on appreciation of mechanics, dynamics, and aesthetics. As you iterate your ideas and test them, try to see how changes in one component can affect the others. You'll start to gain a feel for the subtle interplay and balance involved in game design.

Through mastering these aspects of game design, you can start to create experiences that resonate with players, crafting games that aren't just technically accomplished, but also emotionally engaging, strategically satisfying, and aesthetically captivating. So, step forward into the design process, and let the mechanics, dynamics, and aesthetics of your game spring to life.

Your game design journey is taking shape, and the vistas are just getting breathtaking!

Chapter 6. Developing Your First Game: 2D Concepts

Before you can embark on your journey to developing your first 2D game, you need a solid foundation in a few key areas. In this chapter, we'll dive deep into understanding the basic concepts of 2D game development including game design theory, graphics and animation, sound design, and game programming.

6.1. Understanding Game Design Theory

Every game has a soul, a purpose, a storyline that gives it its very essence. This is where game design theory comes in. It's about the ideas, the concepts, and the rationale that form the base of your game.

The first step of your game development journey should be establishing your game's premise or its 'core loop'. A core loop is an activity or set of activities that players repeat over and over. For example, in the game 'Super Mario Bros', the core loop is: running, jumping, overcoming obstacles, collecting coins, and reaching the end of each level.

Moreover, game design also focuses on user experience (UX). When you're designing your game, remember the player should find it compelling enough to continue playing. Invest time in considering what actions the player will be performing, how these actions fit into the larger narrative of the game, and most importantly, if it's fun!

6.2. Understanding Graphics and Animation

The graphical elements of your 2D game design play a crucial role in getting your players hooked. In 2D game development, you will mostly work with sprites, which are 2D graphics that are integrated into the game world. They can be anything from your characters to the way that fire flickers in your game's environment.

Animating your sprites can bring them to life, making your game more immersive and intriguing. In simple terms, animation is a sequence of images or frames shown in quick succession to create the illusion of movement. For example, a character walking or the flame flickering.

You might want to adopt pixel art – blocks of colored squares, for your game as it is easily manageable, scalable, and doesn't require high-end graphics.

6.3. Understanding Sound Design

Sound design is another important aspect that adds depth to your game. A well-composed background score can create an immersive gaming experience. At the same time, sound effects like footsteps, fight noises, or character-specific phrases could add a realness that engages players.

There are many audio libraries and software that you can use to design your game's sound effects. Some of them are open-source, and others come with a price. It depends on your preference and budget.

6.4. Programming Your First Game

Now, coming to the part that ties everything together, programming.

You'd be using a programming language to define how your game works. There are numerous game engines available that support a variety of different programming languages; take, for example, Unity that supports C#, or Godot that supports GDScript and C#, among others.

A crucial part of programming involves scripting your game logic. This includes controlling how your characters behave, when and how sound effects or music play, how the game responds to player input, and so on.

6.5. Getting Hands-On

Perhaps the best way to learn is by getting hands-on. It's time to create a simple first game - how about a classic game of Pong? You'll need sprites for the paddles and ball, game logic for the ball to bounce and points to be scored, and maybe a nice blip sound effect when the ball hits the paddle.

Start with sketching out the game, its rules, and its presentation. Then, moving onto designing your sprites, animating them and working on the game's soundscape. Lastly, dive into writing the game logic that binds it all together. Remember, success is iterative, so repeat, refine, and rework until you're happy with your game.

One day, with diligence and enthusiasm, you'll fondly look back at this rudimentary game as the start of your successful journey into game development. Happy gaming!

In conclusion, your voyage into 2D game development is bound to be filled with challenges. However, with a good understanding of game design theory, graphics and animation, sound design, and programming, you're well set to take them on. The joy and gratification you derive from seeing your game ideas and creations come to life will undeniably make your journey worthwhile. Just keep making games, keep learning from both successes and failures, and keep pushing boundaries. The gaming world awaits with bated breath, and remember, every great game designer started at zero.

Chapter 7. Enhancing Interaction: The Power of 3D Design

Game development is an intricate process confounding many novice developers, but one of the most pivotal elements, undoubtedly, is 3D design. It's the unique capability of 3D design to emulate reality and elevate the immersive experience in-game that truly sets it apart.

Understanding the Basics of 3D Design in Gaming

Maestros of game design unanimously echo the importance of 3D design, often describing it as the heartbeat of modern game creation. Before we delve in, it's important to comprehend what 3D design is and how it influences gameplay experience.

3D (three-dimensional) design in the context of games circles around creating objects and environments with three-dimensional properties - length, width, and height. Through complex algorithms, drawing techniques, and rendering, designers create a virtual environment that player characters can navigate. These environments can be molded to feature natural landscapes, eerie dungeons, metropolises, or any universe imaginable. The range is unlimited, only bounded by the designer's creativity and technical prowess.

Dissection of a 3D Model

A 3D model follows a structure composed of:

IMPORTANT

- Vertices: They are the coordinates in the 3D space.
- Edges: They're lines connecting the various vertices.

- Faces: Polygonal areas enclosed by the edges.

- Mesh: It represents the complete model, constituted by vertices, edges, and faces.

Underneath, we dive into the nuts and bolts further, exploring the essentials revolving around the creation, manipulation, and rendering of 3D designs.

7.1. The Tools of the Trade: 3D Software

Game designers utilize special software, aptly known as 3D modeling software, to create and design these intricate 3D models and environments. Some popular ones have been Maya, Blender, 3ds Max, Zbrush, and Cinema 4D. Each software has unique features, capabilities, and user interface, hence the choice depends on your needs and workflow.

TIP	Explore different 3D software to find what works best for you. Many come with free trials or open-source variants for beginners to use and learn.

7.2. From Concept to Creation: The Art of Modeling

3D modeling is the process where digital artists create the surface and structure of a 3D object. This art can be roughly broken down into two core methods - Box Modeling and Sculpting.

Box modeling, also called subdivision modeling, begins with a primitive shape that is then refined and edited to form complex shapes. The model's geometry is manipulated at the vertex (singular point), edge (line segment), or polygon level.

In Sculpting, the modeler starts with a digital 'lump of clay', which is then pushed, pulled, added to, and subtracted from, using various tools to create the desired form. This method offers a more tactile sculpting experience and is often used for more organic subjects.

The choice between box modeling and sculpting is not an either-or proposition. Most game artists employ a hybrid approach, using both to make the most of their advantages.

7.3. Texturing: Bringing Your Models to Life

After your model has been formed, the next step is to color and detail it – a process known as texturing. Texturing involves creating a 'skin' for your 3D model, which can bring it to life with colors, patterns, and textures. Designers use textures to display decals, colors, glossiness, and other surface details.

A vital part of texturing is UV mapping – the 3D modeling procedure of making a 2D image representation of your 3D model's surface. The process is known as 'UV' mapping because the XYZ coordinates are replaced by UVW; U and V signify the axis of the 2D texture, while W relates to multiple textures on one surface.

7.4. Lighting: Setting the Mood

Lighting in games works much the same way as in the real world. Light and darkness can be manipulated to create atmospheres, guide gameplay, and display models. The positioning, color, and intensity of the lights can dramatically influence how a scene feels.

7.5. Animation: Breathing Movement into Your Game

The final bow that ties together the package of 3D design is animation. Animation can be used to infuse your models with movement, breathing life into your game world. It involves the manipulation of 3D models so that they appear to move, typically along pre-determined paths or in response to players' actions.

Remember, every step in the process is interconnected. Lighting and movement particularly benefit from a good texture job, and poor models can let down otherwise perfect textures and animations.

Incorporating the power of 3D design in your game development can be challenging, but it promises an immersive and engaging experience for users. Arm yourself with creativity, subdue the technical side of things, and watch your game go from a dream to game-played reality.

Chapter 8. Embracing the Art of Storytelling and Character Development

Storytelling and character development are deeply intertwined. A compelling story is often driven by well-developed characters and vice versa. The nexus between these elements breeds an immersive gaming environment that fascinates and keeps gamers coming back for more.

8.1. Understanding The Art Of Storytelling

Storytelling, at its core, is a communication art that uses a structured narrative to convey a message, evoke feelings, or nurture understanding in an audience. In the context of game design, it leads gamers through various plots, intertwining gameplay mechanics with narratives, and deeply immersing players into the world of the game.

Traditional storytelling consists of two key elements – plot and character. The plot is the sequential series of events that happen to the characters, and the characters are the individuals to whom the events occur. Consequently, a riveting story depends on these elements, and their execution shapes audience perceptions and engagement.

However, storytelling in games differs from traditional media. Interactive by nature, games allow players to influence the story direction, an advantage that should be capitalized in game design. Interactive storytelling can be linear or nonlinear:

1. Linear Storytelling: The plot remains the same regardless of a player's actions. It's a clear and straightforward scripting of events that lead to a definitive conclusion.

2. Nonlinear Storytelling: The plot changes depending on the player's decisions or actions. It adds complexity and variability, enhancing replayability.

8.2. Developing Rich Game Characters

Characters breathe life into the world of the game and are critical conduits for storytelling. They carry the narrative, personify game values, and serve as the player's touchpoint within the game. A well-developed character fosters emotional connections and enriches player experience:

1. Be Consistent: Consistency in character design goes beyond visual elements. It involves maintaining uniformity in character behavior, speech, and reactions throughout the game.

2. Be Relatable: Characters become real when players can relate to them. Create backstories, virtues, vices, or quirks that mirror human reality and fuel empathy.

3. Be Dynamic: Dynamic characters evolve with the plot, learning, and changing from their experiences. Such transformations capture attention and add depth to the narrative.

8.3. Connecting Storytelling To Gameplay

The story serves as the backdrop for gameplay, setting the stage where the action unfolds. It gives context to quests, challenges, or puzzles and influences the way a player interacts within the game.

Gameplay should not just be an event, but part of the story. Every fight, fetch quest, or friendship fostered serves as a narrative beat that advances the larger plot. Plot development should therefore be intertwined with gameplay to maintain the cohesive context of the game world.

8.4. Connecting Character Development to Gameplay

In game-focused narratives, character development often parallels the leveling up system. As the player advances, the character likewise progresses, unlocking new skills, memories, or aspects of their personality. This development can influence gameplay, changing the dynamics of combat or character interactions.

Additionally, games can encourage players to project their personality onto game characters, leading to a more personalized and immersive experience. These player-character connections also drive deeper engagement, resulting in higher player retention.

8.5. Conclusion

The art of storytelling and character development is a massive game design component. By effectively intertwining plot, character, and gameplay, game developers can create rich, engaging experiences that resonate with players and ensure their return. Balancing these elements is a perplexing puzzle. Unraveling it requires creativity, tenacity, and a keen understanding of the target audience's desires.

Chapter 9. The Ins and Outs of Testing and Debugging

Testing and debugging are integral to every aspect of game design. From initial prototypes to release and post-production patches, the process enables developers to find and fix bugs and check the effectiveness and consistency of gameplay elements. It is important to remember that, while mistakes are unavoidable, thorough testing and debugging procedures can mitigate their impact significantly.

9.1. Understanding the Basics of Testing and Debugging

Testing and debugging are two integral steps involved in creating games. Testing is the process where a game is methodically evaluated under controlled conditions to identify faults, inconsistencies, or other potential issues. Once identified, debugging comes into play – the process where these errors are found and fixed in the code.

Extensive testing is crucial to achieving a high-quality game. Players' experiences are said to be directly proportional to the degree and quality of testing. Therefore, to create the best gaming experiences, without flawed gameplay or frustrating crashes, it's necessary to conduct meticulous testing and debugging.

9.2. Importance of A Testing Plan

Developing a testing plan is instrumental for successful testing and debugging. A testing plan primarily describes what to test, how to test, and when to test.

To make a testing plan, you need to identify what aspects of the game need to be tested – game mechanics, user interface, balance, and more. You also need to specify how you're going to test each of these aspects. For a majority of them, manual playtesting would be necessary, but for others, automated testing tools can be used. The plan should also have a timeline for when and how often each part will be tested.

Having clear and comprehensive testing plans not only provides direction and structure to your testing efforts, but it also helps to maximize efficiency and productivity.

9.3. Implementing Automations

Automated testing is a crucial part of the testing and debugging process, particularly for larger scale games. Automated tests are scripts written by developers that run a series of in-game actions over and over to look for unexpected responses. These scripts provide a great way to perform repeated and precise tests that can highlight significant stability issues, crashes, or slowdowns.

For instance, an automatic test could be set up to run a character through the same set of in-game movements thousands of times to check for an elusive crash or to identify any inconsistencies. Automated testing is especially effective for finding errors in multiplayer games where the multitude of variables can compound.

9.4. Ensuring Consistency

Consistency tests are designed to ensure the gameplay is consistent across various platforms and configurations. These tests include platform testing, performance testing, compatibility testing, and load testing.

Platform testing ensures the game runs as intended across multiple platforms. Performance tests verify that the game maintains a consistent frame rate and doesn't slow down under peak gameplay conditions, while compatibility tests scrutinize the game's performance across different hardware configurations. Lastly, load tests verify whether the game can handle high loads, valuable particularly in multiplayer games.

9.5. Testing Gameplay Mechanics

Gameplay mechanics are what constitute the heart of a game. Making sure that your mechanics are working as intended is essential to producing a quality game. Gameplay tests verify the mechanics, rules, and systems within the game. This includes everything from dialogue systems to combat mechanics, and inventory management.

Repetitive tests can be used to test things like random number generators, artificial intelligence routines, physics engines, or other consistent systems within the game.

9.6. User Interface and Accessibility

User Interface (UI) plays an essential role in the player's experience. Testing the UI involves checking menus, controls, HUD, on-screen messages, and all the other ways that the game communicates with the player.

Accessibility, on the other hand, ensures that your game can be enjoyed by a broad range of players, including those with disabilities. This includes options for color-blind players, subtitles for players who are hard of hearing, and the ability to re-map controls for those who may have motor impairments.

9.7. Debugging Processes

Once you have found a bug through testing, you need to formally report it and fix the error. The debugging process typically involves identifying the cause of the bug, locating the faulty code, fixing or rewriting the code, and retesting to ensure the bug has been fully squashed.

Documentation is crucial in this process. Using bug tracking software helps to keep track of identified bugs and their status. Such systems can also be used to prioritize bugs based on factors such as player impact, frequency, and difficulty to fix.

9.8. Post-launch Patching

Game testing and debugging is not just limited to pre-launch phases. Post-launch, games can still reveal unforeseen bugs or issues due to the vast array of player behaviors and system configurations. As such, developers will often continue to patch issues post-launch, using feedback from player experiences, reviews, and forums.

Patching also allows developers the flexibility to tweak game balance, AI behaviors, or even add new content to enhance the player's experience further.

In conclusion, testing and debugging are vital for ensuring a seamless gaming experience. A strategic approach to testing, including a robust plan, the use of automation, consistency checking, gameplay mechanics testing, UI and accessibility assessment, and post-launch patching, coupled with effective debugging procedures, can significantly improve the quality of the game and ensure its success on the market.

Chapter 10. The Role of Community in Game Development

In the exciting ecosystem of game development, the community holds a pivotal role. By influencing game design, inspiring creatives, providing feedback, and fostering a supportive environment, the community acts as both a backbone and a guiding star for game developers. But how exactly does this dynamic work? What aspects of game development does the community impact? And most importantly, how can you, an aspiring game developer, derive value from this community?

10.1. The Community as End-Users

Understanding that the community consists primarily of end-users - the gamers themselves - is essential. These individuals spend countless hours playing, scrutinizing, and discussing games. Turning to them for inputs about user preferences and gameplay experience can prove monumental in shaping a game that appeals to the masses.

It's crucial to actively engage with the gaming community through forums, social media platforms, and multiplayer arenas. Encouraging them to voice their opinions can provide you with an idea about player expectations, helping you tailor your game accordingly. Feedback garnered from these interactions can also help identify potential flaws in your game design or mechanics, paving the way for improvements.

10.2. The Community as a Testing Ground

Game developers often employ the community as an effective testing ground. By involving them in early-access programs, closed betas, and open-source collaborations, developers can accumulate valuable feedback during the development process, fine-tune their games before launch, and ensure high quality and user satisfaction.

But remember, managing a community during public testing can be tricky. It's important to strike a balance between taking constructive criticism on board and remaining true to your original design vision, while also creating an environment that encourages the community to actively participate in the development process.

10.3. The Community as a Source of Inspiration

The community can also serve as a rich source of creative thinking and innovative ideas. Users often express desires for features that haven't yet been implemented in existing games or suggest tweaks to enhance gameplay.

Additionally, the Modding Community – a subset of the larger gaming community that modifies game content – often brings unprecedented ideas to the fore. From unique skins to fresh game modes, these modifications can significantly transform the game, offering new perspectives for game developers.

10.4. Crowdsourcing and the Community

Crowdsourcing within the community can aid in generating funds for your game development project. Platforms like Kickstarter have revolutionized the way games are funded, making the community central to this monetary aspect. In return for their financial contributions, backers often receive exclusive game content or other perks. Successfully leveraging crowdsourced funding requires strong community management skills and honoring your commitments to backers.

10.5. Community as Brand Advocates

An enthusiastic and supportive community can serve as a powerful marketing resource. Word of mouth and user-generated content, like live game streaming, can significantly extend the reach and visibility of your game, effectively acting as free advertising.

But beware, an unsatisfied community can equally harm your game's reputation. Thus, maintaining open communication channels and fostering a positive relationship with your community is paramount.

10.6. The Power of Esports Communities

In recent times, competitive gaming or Esports has gained significant traction. Harnessing the power of the Esports community can contribute towards setting your game apart from the competition. In addition to exposing your game to a wider audience, these communities can also lead to valuable partnerships and endorsement deals.

10.7. In Summary

Effectively leveraging the power of community requires constant engagement, care, and respect for the community members. It can act as a resource, an inspiration, a testing ground, and a marketing force - all rolled into one. By fostering a friendly and cooperative bond with the community, you can make the game development process enjoyable, enriching, and successful. After all, the gaming community is the lifeblood that keeps the gaming industry thriving, and understanding its role in game development is a critical first step along your journey from zero to game designer.

In our upcoming sections, we will dwell deeper into how to manage and nurture an effective gaming community. So, stay tuned!

Chapter 11. Taking the Leap: Building Your Career in Game Design

Stepping into the field of game design can be as thrilling as it is daunting. With an industry that's constantly evolving and opportunities aplenty, charting your career path in game design requires not just talent, but also strategic planning, dedication, and a relentless pursuit of knowledge. This segment aims to equip you with the essential skills, knowledge, and strategies to begin your journey into the realms of game creation.

11.1. Discovering Your Niche

From expansive open-world RPGs to fast-paced battle arenas, from immersive VR experiences to nostalgic 8-bit adventures, game design is a vast landscape brimming with diverse opportunities. It all begins with figuring out your unique niche: What type of games do you want to develop? What sort of experiences are you looking to offer your players? Identifying your niche will help you focus your skills, refine your knowledge, and carve a unique space for yourself in this enormous industry.

You should explore different game genres to identify where your interests lie. Play games that span across a slew of styles and formats - this will not just help you identify your niche but also broaden your game design palette, giving you a holistic understanding of game design possibilities.

11.2. Fundamental Skills

Once you've identified your niche, you need to equip yourself with a host of skills. Game design isn't just about being creatively inclined. It's also about having a range of hard and soft skills that can help you navigate this dynamic landscape.

1. Creative Skills: The crux of being a game designer is having strong creativity. You should have the knack to think out-of-the-box and build immersive worlds that draw gamers in.

2. Technical Skills: This involves understanding different programming languages like C++, Python, or JavaScript. Also, you should familiarize yourself with game development platforms like Unity, Unreal Engine, Godot, or Construct.

3. Artistic Ability: Grasp of artistic fundamentals like drawing, modeling, animation, texturing, and lighting is vital.

4. Analytical Skills: This involves the ability to discern how small changes can influence a player's experience.

5. Team Management: Most games are built by teams, so you need to be an excellent communicator and a team player.

When building these skills, remember that perfection doesn't come overnight. Start with small steps and learn from every experience.

11.3. Academic Journey

Contrary to popular belief, game design does involve considerable academic learning. A host of colleges and universities offer specific courses on game design, and these could be invaluable in refining your skills, understanding industry-standard practices, and getting access to networking opportunities.

Courses range from principles of game design, game art, computer programming, interactive narrative, and more.

However, remember that while academic progression is important, practical experience is equally crucial. Many game designers have built successful careers without formal game design education but through self-learning, online courses, and sheer practice.

11.4. Building Your Portfolio

One of the most crucial elements any game designer needs is a solid portfolio. Your portfolio gives potential employers or collaborators a glimpse into your creativity, technical prowess, unique approach, and versatility.

Remember to include:

1. A collection of your best games,

2. Any notable contributions to game projects,

3. Samples of your work, like sketches or game concepts,

4. Any awards or recognition you've received.

Keeping the portfolio updated with your latest works is key.

11.5. Networking

A significant part of building a successful career in game design revolves around networking. Regular interactions with other designers can provide you with opportunities to learn, collaborate, find mentorship, or gain exposure.

You can explore online forums, attend industry events, or be part of gaming communities.

11.6. Constant Learning

Lastly, remember that game design is a rapidly evolving field. To stay at the top of your game, continuous education is key. Keep up with industry trends, experiment with new technologies, play a range of games, and learn from the designs you admire and those you do not.

Taking a leap into game designing is an incredible journey. At times it can seem overwhelming, but with patience, persistence, and continuous learning, this journey can be a rewarding adventure. Make a career out of your passion, and let's create an unforgettable chapter in the gaming industry!

www.ingramcontent.com/pod-product-compliance
Lightning Source LLC
Chambersburg PA
CBHW071015260726
48661CB00007B/2974